ISLAM & EUROPE:
PEACE, IDENTITY & INTEGRATION

ISLAM & EUROPE

PEACE, IDENTITY & INTEGRATION

ADDRESSES OF HIS HOLINESS
MIRZA MASROOR AHMAD

KHALIFATUL-MASIH V

ISLAM INTERNATIONAL PUBLICATIONS LTD

Islam & Europe: Peace, Identity & Integration

A compilation of keynote addresses
delivered by
His Holiness Mirza Masroor Ahmad
Head of the Worlwide Ahmadiyya Muslim Community
Fifth Successor to the Promised Messiah[as]

Published by:
Islam International Publications Ltd.
Unit 3, Bourne Mill Business Park,
Guildford Road, Farnham, Surrey, GU9 9PS, United Kingdom

© Islam International Publications Limited. 2020

Cover Design by Nauman Hadi

Printed in Great Britain by Bell and Bain Ltd, Glasgow

For more information please visit:
www.alislam.org

ISBN: 978-1-84880-574-3
10 9 8 7 6 5 4 3 2 1

CONTENTS

HIS HOLINESS HAZRAT MIRZA MASROOR AHMAD
KHALIFATUL-MASIH V^{ABA}

ABOUT HIS HOLINESS
MIRZA MASROOR AHMAD

His Holiness, Mirza Masroor Ahmad, Khalifatul-Masih V^{aba}, is the supreme head of the worldwide Ahmadiyya Muslim Community. He is the Fifth Khalifah of the Promised Messiah and Reformer, Hazrat Mirza Ghulam Ahmad^{as} of Qadian.

His Holiness was born on September 15, 1950 in Rabwah, Pakistan to the late Mirza Mansoor Ahmad and the late Nasirah Begum Ahmad. Upon completing his Masters Degree in Agricultural Economics in 1977 from the Agriculture University in Faisalabad, Pakistan, he formally dedicated his life to the service of Islam. He was sent to Ghana in 1977 where, for several years, he served as a principal of various Ahmadiyya Muslim schools.

Later, when His Holiness returned to Pakistan, he served in various capacities at the Headquarters of the Ahmadiyya Muslim Community in Rabwah.

Elected to the lifelong position of Khalifah (Caliph) of the Ahmadiyya Muslim Community on 22nd April 2003, His Holiness serves as the worldwide spiritual and administrative head of an international religious organization with tens of millions of members spread across more than 200 countries.

Since being elected Khalifah, His Holiness has led a worldwide campaign to convey the peaceful message of Islam, through all forms of print and digital media. Under his leadership, national branches of the Ahmadiyya Muslim Community have launched campaigns that reflect the true and peaceful teachings of Islam. Ahmadi Muslims the world over are engaged in grass-roots efforts to distribute millions of 'peace' leaflets to Muslims and non-Muslims alike, host interfaith and peace symposia and organize exhibitions of the Holy Qur'an to present its true and noble message. These campaigns have received worldwide media coverage and demonstrate that Islam champions peace, loyalty to one's country of residence and service to humanity.

In 2004, His Holiness launched the annual National Peace Symposium in which guests from all walks of life come together to exchange ideas on the promotion of peace and harmony. Each year, the symposium attracts many serving ministers, parliamentarians, politicians, religious leaders and other dignitaries.

His Holiness has travelled globally to promote and facilitate service to humanity. Under the leadership of His Holiness, the Ahmadiyya Muslim Community has built a number of schools and hospitals that provide excellent education and healthcare in remote parts of the world.

His Holiness strives to establish peace at every level of society. He constantly advises members of the Ahmadiyya Muslim Community to carry out a 'jihad' (or struggle) of the self to strive to reform individually, which is the true and biggest form of 'jihad,' so that every Ahmadi Muslim can first establish peace on an individual level, and then be enabled to also help others find peace.

At an individual and collective level, on local, national and international platforms, His Holiness is striving to advise all others of the practical means of establishing peace, based on the true teachings of Islam.

His Holiness, Mirza Masroor Ahmad[aba] currently resides in Islamabad, Tilford (Surrey). As spiritual leader of Ahmadi Muslims all over the world, he vigorously champions the cause of Islam through a refreshing message of peace and compassion.

FOREWORD

The current socio-economic situation in Europe has pushed the sentiments of nations towards the pre-world war *'ideals'* that are seldom achieved. Nationalism has not only established a strong footing the world over but is beginning to normalise its fiercer sides. In such times, as history has taught us, are mentalities which alienate anyone other than *'us'* forged leading to a divided society.

The voice of His Holiness Mirza Masroor Ahmad – Khalifatul-Masih V is key in healing such divisions. This book brings together 4 addresses of His Holiness delivered in Germany, France and Holland in 2019 on the themes of establishing a harmonious society based upon Islamic principles - dispelling the belief that Islamic teachings are not suitable for 21st century Europe.

The words of His Holiness resonate in such profound understanding and perception of what is required to alleviate the tensions that exist between the peoples of a nation, that millions flock to seek his guidance on a colossal spectrum of issues. For example in his address in Berlin (see chapter *Islam & Europe: A Clash of Civilisations?*) he states: *'As a Muslim leader, I believe you should protect your heritage and culture by focusing your energies on arresting the decline in religion and bringing people back towards faith and belief, whether that be Christianity, Judaism or any other. It should not be that in the name of advancement, those values and moral standards that have been part of society for many centuries are suddenly abandoned.'*

Similarly, in the address delivered at the inauguration of the Baitul-Afiyyat Mosque in Almere, Holland he explains the role of a Mosque as being the centre of peace, where all people can gather and remember their Creator. Such a call for universal solidarity, without having to compromise religious beliefs, is arguably the best definition of integration we find.

His Holiness calls for compassion, tolerance and kindness to be adopted at all levels of society so that we can avert the many disasters that await the human race.

We hope that the reader will benefit from this book, for it holds a message that shall be apt and pertinent for times to come.

The Publishers
September 2020

SPEECHES

THE NEED FOR OUTWARD AND INNER PEACE

ANNUAL CONVENTION HOLLAND
28 SEPTEMBER 2019

His Holiness Mirza Masroor Ahmad[aba] graced the 39th Annual Convention of the Ahmadiyya Muslim Community Holland. Over the course of the Convention he delivered addresses and met with many Ahmadis as well as guests.

> **“** *Islam instructs Muslims to emulate, to the best of their abilities, the attributes of God and so the Prophet of Islam (peace and blessings be upon him) stated repeatedly that his followers must be compassionate and considerate and strive to impart peace to others. A golden principle given by the Founder of Islam (peace and blessings of Allah be upon him) is that a true Muslim should like for others, what he likes for himself.*

Preface

On Saturday 28 September 2019, the Worldwide Head of the Ahmadiyya Muslim Community, the Fifth Khalifah (Caliph), His Holiness, Hazrat Mirza Masroor Ahmad[aba] addressed an audience of more than 125 dignitaries and guests on the second day of the 39th Annual Convention of the Ahmadiyya Muslim Community in Holland.

In this address His Holiness begins by outlining the current state of the world in terms of peace - both at a personal and national level. Mental health is a key area that he speaks about with an emphasis on establishing a relationship with God as means of alleviating such distresses. Furthermore, he explains that the lack of true justice being dispensed by many nations is a key reason why strife exists today. He also draws on Islamic history and teachings to demonstrate that Islam is a religion of peace and tolerance, and that the belief that it is due to Islamic beliefs that today's turmoil exists is unfounded.

THE NEED FOR OUTWARD
AND INNER PEACE

All distinguished guests, *Assalamo Alaikum Wa Rahmatullahe Wa Barakatohu* – peace and blessings of Allah be upon you all.

First of all, I would like to thank all of our guests, who have accepted our invitation and joined us here today, even though much has been said against Islam and its founder in recent years. In fact, a concerted attempt has been made to spread hatred and misinformation about Islam and to malign the character of the Holy Prophet Muhammad (peace and blessings of Allah be upon him). In light of this, your attendance at this religious event, hosted by a Muslim community, testifies to your open hearts and broad-mindedness and for this, I can only commend and thank you. I pray that this generous and tolerant spirit always remains within you and that it spreads much further afield so that the people of all communities can live together in peace and with a spirit of mutual love and respect.

We, Ahmadi Muslims, firmly believe that religion is a personal matter for every individual. It is a matter of the heart and no one has the right to speak ill of the beliefs of other people. No one should mock what others consider sacred, because treating other people with derision and contempt can only lead to pain and suffering and create division. Conversely, tolerance and mutual respect are the cornerstones through which we can build a peaceful and harmonious society.

As I have mentioned, the character of the Holy Prophet of Islam (peace and blessings of Allah be upon him) has long been slandered and distorted in the non-Muslim world. Here in Holland as well, certain people have taken the lead in inciting hatred against Islam and making utterly false and horrific assertions about the Holy Quran and the Holy Prophet Muhammad (peace and blessings of Allah be upon him).

In this regard, I shall, in the short time available, speak about Islam's true teachings and the character of its founder (peace and blessings of Allah be upon him). However, before proceeding, I would like to speak, more generally, about what constitutes peace and why it is so important.

Undoubtedly, at a personal level, peace is something we all desire, whilst at a broader level, it is something that different nations and communities claim to aspire towards. However, what is peace and why do we need it? In my view, there are two types of peace. There is outward peace and inner peace. Often, at a superficial level, people can appear to be happy and content. Yet, though they have outward peace, they remain bereft of inner peace. For example, powerful and influential people often speak about developing peace and they personally possess all the trappings and comforts of the world.

Nevertheless, many admit that they remain in search of peace of mind and are consumed by tension and vexation. From a purely external and material point of view, they have all that they need, yet their minds remain plagued by anxiety and their hearts remain unfulfilled. Thus, the reality is that until a person attains inner peace, their material comforts are worthless. Simply put, the one thing money cannot buy is inner peace.

For example, imagine the case of an affluent mother, who has riches beyond her needs, but her child becomes lost. Despite having every possible worldly comfort, she will remain frantic and desperate until she finds her child.

Sadly, in both the developed and developing world, mental health issues are on the rise. In rich countries, increasing numbers of people are committing suicide, suffering from breakdowns or depression, even though they are relatively strong in financial terms. Unsurprisingly, a lack of inner-peace is also common amongst the weaker and vulnerable members of society, who cannot fulfil their basic needs, and who desperately yearn for the comforts available to others.

Thus, frustration and inner-turmoil is palpable amongst the rich and the poor.

On one side, affluent people, who have all they need in material terms, remain bereft of inner peace. At the other end of the spectrum, the poor and needy are plagued by their circumstances and crave the comfortable lives of others.

People may have different goals or desires, and they may be poles apart in terms of their material state, but they are united in their failure to attain inner-contentment.

In today's world, critics are quick to blame religion and particularly Islam, for the problems of the world. Yet, many people who are suffering from inner-torment and unrest are those who live a purely secular existence and so their problems cannot be blamed on Islam or any other religion.

As a religious leader, I firmly believe that instead of being the cause of today's problems, religion is the answer and from an Islamic perspective, the solution is quite simple.

The Prophet of Islam (peace and blessings be upon him) taught that true peace of mind requires for a person to recognise God Almighty and to develop a connection with Him because, according to Islam, one of the attributes of God Almighty is that He is the 'Source of Peace'.

He desires for His creation to live peacefully, irrespective of any differences of religion or belief. Furthermore, the Holy Prophet Muhammad (peace and blessings of Allah be upon him) taught that Allah the Almighty is the provider and sustainer of all creation. He does not just provide for Muslims, but His grace encompasses all humanity, be they Christians, Hindus, Sikhs, Jews or the people of other faiths and beliefs and indeed of those who have no faith and deny His existence.

Islam instructs Muslims to emulate, to the best of their abilities, the attributes of God[1] and so the Prophet of Islam (peace and blessings be upon him) stated repeatedly that his followers must be compassionate and considerate and strive to impart peace to others.[2] A golden principle given by the Founder of Islam (peace and blessings of Allah be upon him) is that a true Muslim should like for others, what he likes for himself.[3] I believe that this simple and profound point, if acted upon, not just by Muslims, but by all people, is the means for everlasting peace in society. No doubt, everyone desires peace for themselves and their loved ones, but most people will be lying if they claim that they want their opponents and competitors to have peace and to live with contentment.

Yet this is the standard of nobility and generosity of spirit that Islam requires. It is a religion and teaching that promotes selflessness and urges humans to discard all traces of selfishness. The principle given by Islam's Prophet (peace and blessings of Allah be upon him) is that a person should be open-hearted and pure of mind. Instead of desiring only the best for himself, a person should desire the same for others as well. Sadly, in today's world, we tend to see the opposite.

Modern society is consumed by self-interest and greed. Disorder, conflict and warfare are on the rise and the principles of equity and justice are being consistently discarded. This is illustrated by the foreign policies of many powerful and rich countries. It has been a constant theme of modern history that dominant powers have sent their armies to distant lands, on the pretext of establishing peace, but time has proven that their real objective has been to protect and enhance their vested interests. During such conflicts, if just one of their soldiers dies there is an outpouring of grief and they pledge to take revenge. Yet, when their bombs or munitions cause the death of hundreds or even thousands of innocent civilians – including defenceless women and children - they remain silent and do not express any hint of regret or remorse.

The consequences of such injustice are extremely damaging and far-reaching. The local people see that their lives are deemed to be of far less worth and value than the lives of those who are from powerful nations.

As they observe the stark double standards and the lack of humanity, they become overcome by frustration, anger and resentment and their emotions threaten to boil over at any time.

The peace and security of such nations lie in ruins but the rest of the world would be foolish to think that they will not be affected; rather, the world is now so inter-connected that the ramifications of hostilities in one part of the world, are bound to spread beyond borders and we have seen many examples of this in recent years. Hence, if we genuinely desire peace, whether in our personal lives or at a collective level, the pivotal point is that we should like for others what we like for ourselves. As I said before, this simple principle is the foundation for true peace in the world.

In terms of religion, the Holy Prophet Muhammad (peace and blessings of Allah be upon him) taught that developing true peace requires for mankind to turn towards God Almighty, who is the Source of Peace, the Noble and the Pure and to try to emulate His attributes. This means that human beings should set aside their personal interests in the pursuit of peace and ensure that their motivations are pure at all times.

Certainly, much of the division prevalent in the world today is because the underlying intentions of the parties involved are not innocent or honest. There are clear contradictions between their words and deeds and there can never be peace if there is disharmony between what a person says and what he does. Every government and every political leader - be they from the United States, China, Russia, European countries, the Muslim world or elsewhere - routinely condemn warfare and bloodshed. However, the reality is that their opposition to such matters tends to remain limited to their interests and their people. Their cries in favour of the rule of law, justice and human rights are all too often rendered hollow when their interests are at stake. If they are attacked or their rights are usurped, they express blind fury and indignation at the injustice, yet they are themselves guilty of targeting weaker nations and exploiting civil wars or conflicts within other countries for their own benefit.

Instead of calling the different parties to the negotiating table and establishing fair and honest dialogue, major powers have habitually interfered in the conflicts of other countries by arming or funding whichever side supports their interests. They are pouring petrol on an open flame and the result is that innocent people, including women, children and the elderly, are losing their lives and observing the torment of their families. Cities, towns and villages are being ravaged and torn asunder. The only possible result is an upsurge in frustration and resentment amongst the local people and this is something that has been all too apparent in war-torn Muslim countries in recent years. Can those external powers, who prioritise their own interests, really claim to be facilitating peace? Furthermore, can the critics of Islam continue to lay the blame for the lack of peace in the world at Islam's door? Can they continue to hold the Prophet of Islam (peace and blessings of Allah be upon him) responsible for the injustices that are taking place today?

Let it be clear that the state of unrest in the world, whether in Muslim countries or otherwise, has nothing to do with the teachings of Islam; rather, such turmoil is based on the vested interests and selfish ways of certain leaders or corrupt governments on the one side and rebel, insurgent or separatist groups on the other.

It is caused by the brutal acts of terrorist and extremist groups who seek only enrichment or power. The centre of today's disorder may well be Muslim countries, but no one can deny that non-Muslim countries have inflamed the situation, rather than resolve it.

It may be claimed that Islamic teachings have motivated extremists and terrorists, but let it be crystal clear that nothing could be further from the truth. As I said, the Prophet of Islam (peace and blessings of Allah be upon him) taught that Allah the Almighty is the Source of Peace and the Provider and Sustainer of all mankind. Indeed, this has been mentioned in the the first chapter of the Holy Quran. Thus, how could it be possible for him to promote intolerance or to sow the seeds of division in society? Rather, throughout his life, he promoted inter-faith harmony and emphasised the need for peace at every level of society - from the basic domestic family unit all the way to international relations. This was not just his teaching, but was also his practice.

From the outset, the Holy Prophet of Islam (peace and blessings of Allah be upon him) conveyed a message of peace and promoted a tolerant and inclusive society. He proclaimed that

God Almighty desired for all people, irrespective of their ethnic background or beliefs, to live in peace and for human values to be recognised and upheld.

It is often alleged that the early Muslims engaged in warfare or were intolerant of the beliefs of others. Yet a fair-minded review of Islamic history proves that these are completely unjust and false accusations. When Islam was founded, the early Muslims were themselves the victims of merciless persecution in Makkah. Some were brutally martyred, others were savagely tortured but the Muslims remained patient and never retaliated.

After bearing the most horrific imaginable cruelties, some of the vulnerable Muslims migrated to the land known today as Ethiopia. Yet still, the opponents of Islam did not let them live in peace; rather they followed them and presented themselves before the King of the land and pleaded with him to banish the Muslims and force them to return to Makkah so they could continue to persecute them and ensure that Islam did not spread.

The disbelievers of Makkah told the King that the Muslims had established a new faith and had condemned idol worship. They claimed the Muslims spread disorder and disturbed the peace of society.

Upon being instructed by the King to present their defence, the Muslims declared their belief in the One God, who was the Creator of all creation. They worshipped Him alone, but at the same time, sought peace with all people and communities and believed that people of different faiths and beliefs should respect one another.

They expressed their belief that the mighty and rich should

not trample upon the rights of the weak and underprivileged, whilst the poor and deprived should not bear hatred for those who were better off.

The King asked the disbelievers if the Muslims had ever waged war, whether they lied, if they broke their pledges or incited rebellion. In reply, the opponents of Islam were forced to admit that the Muslims were innocent of all charges.

Despite their hatred for the Prophet of Islam (peace and blessings be upon him) and his followers and despite their intense desire to finish Islam, the people of Makkah testified to the fact that the Founder of Islam (peace and blessings be upon him) had never spoken an untruth, had never broken a promise and nor had he ever acted with cruelty or injustice.

They were forced to admit that the Holy Prophet of Islam (peace and blessings of Allah be upon him) and his followers were those who only ever sought to spread love and affection in society and who peacefully propagated their belief in the Unity of God.

At all times, the Prophet of Islam (peace and blessings of Allah be upon him) remained patient, even in the face of the most cruel and barbaric oppression.

He turned only to God Almighty to share his pain and so it is mentioned in the Holy Quran that during prayer, the Holy Prophet Muhammad (peace and blessings be upon him) spoke of his grief that he called his people towards peace and prosperity and yet they responded with brutal and incessant cruelty.[4]

Despite their brutalities, during the Makkan period, the Prophet of Islam (peace and blessings be upon him) never raised his sword against those who persecuted the Muslims, nor did he ever stop cooperating with the authorities of Makkah or incite any form of revolt.

The patience of the Muslims was based on the command of Allah the Almighty, which is mentioned in chapter 25, verse 64 of the Holy Quran. Addressing the Muslims in this verse, Allah the Almighty said:

"And the servants of the Gracious God are those who walk on the earth in a dignified manner, and when the ignorant address them, they say, 'Peace!'"

Hence, the Holy Quran reassured the Muslims and counselled them to be patient no matter how much they were provoked or tormented. In the face of adversity and hatred, they were to respond by offering peace to their enemies and opponents.

Consequently, where the early Muslims were tortured, vilified and maligned, they remained patient on the command of God Almighty. Disregarding a natural inclination for revenge and living up to the standard of liking for others what you like for yourself, the Muslims sought peace for their enemies. It was not just a temporary peace the Muslims desired for others, rather an everlasting peace. Thus, in chapter 10, verse 26, Allah the Almighty has stated:

"And Allah calls to the abode of peace…"

This verse makes it clear that Muslims were instructed to

spare no effort in promoting a permanent state of peace and harmony and to bring people together. Yet the bitter persecution continued for years and finally, when their cruelties exceeded all bounds, the Prophet of Islam (peace and blessings be upon him) and his followers migrated to the city of Medina.

Still, the opponents of Islam did not let them live in peace; rather, the disbelievers of Makkah pursued them and soon waged war against the Muslims. Only then, after years of bearing hateful persecution, and after having been driven out of their homes, did God Almighty permit the Muslims to respond with force and to defend themselves.

Here, it is very important to note that permission to fight back was not given just to defend Islam or Muslims; rather, the Holy Quran states in chapter 22, verses 40-41 that permission to fight back was given to defend the institution of religion and universal freedom of belief, as those were the real targets of the opponents of Islam.

It should also be clarified that the Holy Prophet of Islam (peace and blessings of Allah be upon him) instructed his followers to abide by the strictest possible rules of engagement. For example, he ensured that prisoners of war were treated with compassion and freed wherever possible.

He instructed that no child, woman, elderly or sick person was to be targeted, nor were places of worship or religious leaders to be attacked. Further, he instructed that if the opposing side even hinted towards reconciliation their gesture was to be immediately accepted, so that no opportunity for peace was lost.[5]

It is also of note that, where it is commonly suggested that the early Muslims were belligerent or blood-thirsty, today several Western and non-Muslim historians admit that this is wholly inaccurate. In fact, their research shows that the number of people who lost their lives in all of the wars fought in the period of early Islam was a fraction compared to the numbers of people who died at the hands of single bombs in the modern era.[6] Therefore, rather than seeking conflict or fostering hatred, Islam has only ever instructed Muslims to knock down the walls of hatred that divide mankind and to build bridges of love and compassion in order to unite it. In short, at every level of society, and across all communities and peoples, Muslims have a duty to spread peace and the fundamental reason for this, as I have already mentioned, is that the very first chapter of the Holy Quran states:

"All praise belongs to Allah, Lord of all the worlds." [7]

Accordingly, where God Almighty is the Provider and Sustainer for all mankind, it simply not possible for true Muslims to bear hatred or ill-will towards their fellow creation; rather, our hearts can only be filled with sentiments of love, compassion and sympathy for others.

Of course, as practicing Muslims, we have our religious beliefs. We believe that God is One and that it is our duty to turn to Him and to worship Him alone. Yet, we also firmly abide by the timeless precept of the Holy Quran that there should be no compulsion in religion. As I said before, religion is, and always will be, a matter of the heart and a personal matter for each individual. The very meaning of the word Islam is *peace* and there are many verses in the Quran that make it categorically clear that Muslims must be peaceful and show love and respect to others.

How could it be that when such a peaceful teaching was revealed to the Prophet of Islam (peace and blessings of Allah be upon him) that he himself would violate its teachings?

Honest and fair historians testify to the fact that the Holy Prophet of Islam (peace and blessings of Allah be upon him) never inflicted any cruelty or usurped the rights of other people. At every juncture, he taught peace, forbearance and fulfilling the rights of mankind and certainly, his teachings are our inspiration. We proudly proclaim to be the followers of that noble Prophet (peace and blessings of Allah be upon him) who the Holy Quran declared as a mercy for mankind.

This is the reason that the Ahmadiyya Muslim Community raises the slogan of Love for All, Hatred for None. At this time of strife and division, our message is that all nations and all people must urgently strive for peace.

The fierce critics of Islam should recognise that instead of targeting their bile and venom towards Islam and its noble Prophet (peace and blessings be upon him), they should eradicate the traces of bias, prejudice and self-interest. Otherwise, disorder and hatred in the world will continue to escalate. Frustrations and anger amongst those Muslims, who are uneducated or ignorant of the true teachings of their religion, will rise to the surface. Not only amongst the Muslim community, but across society, wherever young people are left hopeless and frustrated, they become easy prey for hateful clerics or extremists who poison their minds.

We must guard against this, otherwise, the bitter cycle of hatred that has darkened the modern world, will continue to turn. Peace within Muslim societies, and in the wider world, will become an ever more distant dream.

As I said at the outset, it is the need of the time that we all join together and instead of inveighing against one another's religious sentiments, we join forces and work towards building a better future for our children and future generations.

Let us set aside our differences and work faithfully towards developing true and sustainable peace in the world. Let us respect one another and strive to build a better society founded upon principles of unity and the common good.

May Allah the Almighty enable us to do so – *Ameen.*

A BEACON OF LIGHT – SPREADING COMPASSION TO ALL

INAUGURAL RECEPTION FOR THE BAITUL AFIYAT MOSQUE
ALMERE, HOLLAND
1 OCTOBER 2019

His Holiness Mirza Masroor Ahmad unveiling the plaque at the inauguration of the Baitul Afiyat Mosque. His Holiness delivered the keynote address at the ceremony that followed. The reception was attended by many local dignitaries and members of the Ahmadiyya Muslim Community.

In the keynote address His Holiness spoke about the role of a Mosque as being a centre of peace for the local community and responsibilities of Ahmadi Muslims in discharging the rights of neighbours.

Preface

On 1 October 2019, the Worldwide Head of the Ahmadiyya Muslim Community, the Fifth Khalifah (Caliph), His Holiness, Hazrat Mirza Masroor Ahmad[aba] inaugurated the Baitul Afiyat Mosque (name translates to The House of Peace and Security) in Almere, Holland. Upon arrival, His Holiness officially inaugurated the Mosque by unveiling a commemorative plaque and offering a silent prayer in thanks to God Almighty. His Holiness led the Zuhr and Asr prayers at the Mosque and also fielded questions from various media outlets in a press conference. Later, a special reception, attended by around 80 dignitaries and guests, was held to mark the opening of the mosque in which the keynote address was delivered by His Holiness.

In this brief address His Holiness speaks about the objectives behind building a Mosque as explained in the Holy Qur'an and the conduct of the Holy Prophet Muhammad[sas]. In great depth, he lays out the duties that local Muslims now have through the presence of a Mosque - whereas, they are obliged to congregate to worship God five times a day, they now also have a duty to uphold the peace and harmony of Almere.

A BEACON OF LIGHT –
SPREADING COMPASSION
TO ALL

All distinguished guests, *Assalamo Alaikum Wa Rahmatullahe Wa Barakatohu* - peace and blessings of Allah be upon you all. First of all, I would like to thank all of you for accepting our invitation and joining us at the opening of our new Mosque here in Almere.

In today's world, many people living in the Western world harbour suspicions about Islam and Muslims. In fact, it is no exaggeration to suggest that many people fear the religion of Islam and its followers. Hence, the fact that you have accepted our invitation, proves that you are open-hearted people and aspire to forge bonds of friendship between the people of different communities and beliefs. It illustrates your desire for inter-faith dialogue and shows you recognise the importance of upholding human values. I sincerely appreciate your gesture and I assure you that our faith teaches us that religion is a matter of the heart and it is for each individual to determine his or her own path, free from any form of coercion. In this regard, the Holy Quran explicitly states that there should be no compulsion in matters of religion.[1]

The inauguration of a mosque is a purely Islamic function and it will be of no surprise to you that we, Ahmadi Muslims, have an emotional connection and deep affiliation to our mosques. Consequently, it is a cause of sincere joy and profound emotion for us that Allah the Almighty has enabled us to build this mosque here in this city, where we can join together for the worship of the One God, in the way that He has taught us.

However, all of you, who are our guests, have no such emotional bond to this mosque, but have still made the effort to participate in today's event and this proves that you are kind, generous and tolerant people. In addition, it shows that you want to increase your knowledge about Islam and learn about the objectives and reasons for which we have built this mosque. For this, I also commend you - because taking the time to learn about the faiths and beliefs of others is a crucial way of knocking down the barriers that divide us and exposing those myths that often cultivate unnecessary anxiety and trepidation.

Certainly, it is a cause of extreme regret to me and to all peace-loving Muslims, that in non-Muslim countries, there is widespread fear of Islam and many people believe that Muslims and mosques are good for nothing, apart from causing problems and undermining the peace and security of society. However, the reality is the opposite and so to alleviate any apprehensions that may exist amongst the local community, I shall now briefly mention the core purposes of mosques, so that you can all better understand what this new mosque represents.

A primary objective of a mosque is the worship of the One God and so mosques are a place where Muslims join together to bow down and prostrate before God Almighty.

A second crucial purpose of a mosque is to be a place for Muslims to strengthen their mutual relations and to develop unity amongst the community members.

The third pivotal objective for any mosque is to be a means of introducing non-Muslims to the teachings of Islam and to fulfil the rights of the wider society. It is to provide a platform and venue from which Muslims can join together to fulfil the rights of their neighbours and the wider society, regardless of creed, caste or colour.

Let it be clear that any mosque, which does not serve as a beacon of peace and sympathy for mankind and from where, neither the rights of God Almighty or His creation are fulfilled, is nothing but a hollow and empty shell. Even a cursory glance of Islamic history proves this to be true.

During the time of the Holy Prophet of Islam (peace and blessings of Allah be upon him), a so-called mosque was erected with the intention of causing mischief and sowing seeds of division within society. It was built to ignite the flames of hatred amongst Muslims and also to trigger hostilities between Muslims and other communities, notably the Jewish community. As a result, it is recorded in the Holy Quran that Allah the Almighty instructed the Holy Prophet (peace and blessings of Allah be upon him) to demolish the mosque, because it had been built with ill-intent.[2] Therefore, the mosque was razed to the ground.

As I said, this incident has been mentioned in the Holy Quran and so will forever serve as a solemn warning and reminder for Muslims. It illustrates that if a mosque does not serve as a centre of peace, where people join to fulfil the rights of their fellow beings and instead serves as a breeding ground for extremism or inciting dissent, it can never fulfil its real purpose or be deemed a true mosque.

A mosque's objectives can only be fulfilled when the worshippers enter the mosque with a firm intention to worship Allah the Almighty and to work for the betterment of humanity. A mosque's purpose can only be fulfilled when the worshippers are infused with a spirit of selflessness, humility and true sympathy and love for all mankind.

Another thing I wish to make clear is that a mosque is a purely religious and spiritual house of worship and should remain free from materialism and clear of anything through which the peace of society is jeopardised. All such activities are utterly prohibited by Islam and the Founder of Islam (peace and blessings be upon him) expressed hatred for such things. It is only permitted to hold those events or gatherings within mosques that encourage the worship of the One God or which peacefully convey Islam's teachings or which serve to fulfil the needs of humanity. Thus, when we build mosques, where we join together for the worship of God Almighty five times a day, and where we hold religious events to enhance our moral and spiritual development, we also hold regular events and establish schemes to serve our neighbours and the wider society.

We devise plans through which we can help the poor and

needy and fulfil the rights of orphans and provide aid and assistance to the vulnerable and deprived members of society.

With the Grace of Allah, to further such efforts, we have established an international charity, Humanity First and from a community level, we hold various charity events across the world throughout the year. For example, in Africa, when we build mosques, apart from introducing the teachings of Islam to others, we strive to help the local people, irrespective of their ethnic or religious backgrounds. We build hospitals, clinics and schools, where all people are welcome. In reality, the majority of the students and patients who attend our schools and hospitals are not members of our community. Also for the sake of serving humanity, and with the sole objective of helping those who are under-privileged, we have established a humanitarian relief project providing water in remote villages and towns of Africa. Our engineers dig boreholes and install water pumps, which provide clean and portable drinking water to the local people. You cannot imagine, until you see it with your own eyes, how the local people, who had no concept of clean water, are overcome with emotion and unbridled joy when they see it flowing from their taps for the very first time. The innocent children, who have been born into destitution and extreme poverty, cannot contain their excitement and wonder. For generations, the local people were forced to travel miles on a daily basis, with vessels or buckets rested on their heads, in order to acquire pond-water for their domestic use. Even that water, for which they had to struggle so much, was invariably contaminated and the cause of many diseases and illnesses. Given this, when those desperate people see fresh and clean water it is as if they have attained all the treasures of the world.

Accordingly, we believe that if a Muslim desires to fulfil the rights of the worship of God Almighty and fulfil the rights of a mosque then he or she must fulfil the rights of mankind. For Muslims, serving God and serving His creation are intrinsically linked. If a Muslim, God forbid, causes pain or distress to other people and fails to show compassion, then, even if they are regular in the worship of God, their prayers and supplications are futile and utterly worthless. Indeed, in chapter 107, verses 3-7 of the Holy Quran, Allah the Almighty states:

"…the one who drives away the orphan, and urges not the feeding of the poor. So woe to those who pray, but are unmindful of their prayers. They only like to be seen of men."

Because they are not discharging their duties towards mankind, their prayers are not accepted. Here, Allah the Almighty has cursed those who pray to him, but fail to fulfil the rights of the weak and needy and He has declared that their prayers will never be accepted. Their worship and entry into a mosque is nothing but a sham and an empty gesture. The Holy Quran is very clear that their prayers are meaningless and their hypocritical ways will lead only to their humiliation and despair.

Consequently, a mosque not only draws our attention to fulfilling the rights of God, but also of fulfilling the rights of mankind and the importance of serving humanity.

When these are the core objectives of true mosques, there

should be no reason for any of you to fear this mosque.

Time and time again, Islam has laid great stress upon caring for one's neighbours and fulfilling their rights. For example, where chapter 4, verse 37 of the Holy Quran calls on Muslims to show love and compassion to their parents and families, it also calls on them to fulfil the needs of the vulnerable members of society and special mention is made towards fulfilling the rights of one's neighbours.

Muslims are taught to love and protect their neighbours, whether they have personal relations with them or not, and to be ever ready to help them in their times of need. Furthermore, the definition of a neighbour in Islam is extremely vast. It includes a person's work colleagues, subordinates and travel companions. It includes not only those people who live in the immediate vicinity but comprises the entire neighbourhood. Indeed, the Holy Prophet of Islam (peace and blessings of Allah be upon him) said that a person's neighbours include at least the forty houses around him.[3] Thus, it can be said that all the people of this city are the neighbours of this mosque or of people who worship at this mosque. Regardless of whether our neighbours are Muslims or non-Muslims, it is our religious duty to care for them, to fulfil their rights and to ensure we do not cause any problems or difficulties for them. This is not a favour on our part but our basic religious duty. In fact, the Prophet of Islam (peace and blessings of Allah be upon him) said that Allah the Almighty had emphasised the importance of discharging the rights of one's neighbours so fervently to him that he began to think that perhaps they would be included amongst a person's rightful inheritors.[4]

In short, now this mosque has been built, our obligation to worship God Almighty has not only increased but, in parallel, our responsibility to serve the local community and to contribute positively to the local society has increased manifold. The local Ahmadi Muslims will consider all the people in this city as their neighbours and recognise that they have many rights over them and will strive to fulfil them to the best of their abilities. Whenever any of you require our help, we pledge to be there to aid and assist, in whatever way we can.

I am confident that the local Ahmadi Muslims will take extremely seriously their obligations towards the local society and will always strive to contribute positively to this city and to be faithful and loyal citizens, who care passionately about their local community.

In light of this, I would also take this opportunity to remind the local Ahmadi Muslims that they must always display the highest moral standards and follow the true teachings of Islam and serve their local community. Through their piety and heartfelt concern for their fellow beings, they should remove any lingering fears or misconceptions of Islam that may exist amongst some members of the local society.

God Willing, I am sure that now this mosque has opened the relations between our community and the wider public will become ever closer and the ties of friendship between us will continue to strengthen forevermore. I am sure that a spirit of love and mutual affection will continue to grow and you will come to see this mosque as a symbol of peace and goodwill for all mankind.

At this time, more than ever before, it is incumbent upon all of us – whether Muslim or non-Muslim - to work together for the cause of peace, and to set aside our religious differences, and unite in the name of humanity, and work towards the betterment of our nation and strive to bring peace in the world.

May Allah the Almighty grant humanity the ability and wisdom to do so.

At the end, I pray that this mosque proves to be an everlasting beacon of light radiating peace, love and humanity in all directions – *Ameen*. With these words, I would like to thank you all once again for joining us on this auspicious occasion. Thank you very much.

ISLAM - SAFEGUARDING RIGHTS AND FREEDOMS

ANNUAL CONVENTION FRANCE
5 OCTOBER 2019

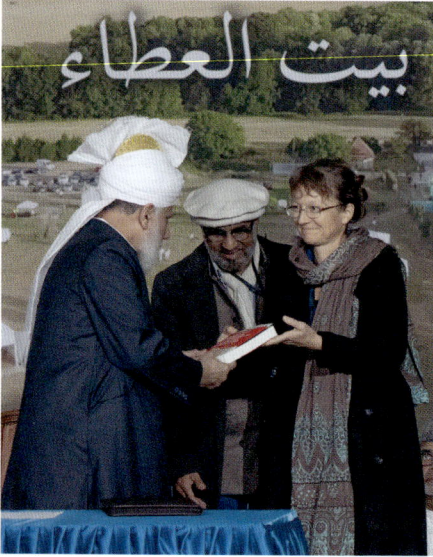

A few dignitaries briefly spoke prior to the keynote address of His Holiness in which they commended the efforts of the Ahmadiyya Muslim Community in the promotion of peace including the Mayor of Trie-Chateau.

In the photograph to the left Dr Katrin Langewiesche presents her book to Hazrat Khalifatul-Masih V.

"

The true teachings of Islam have nothing to do with terrorism and extremism; rather, Islam is a religion of peace, love, tolerance and reconciliation. The word 'Islam' literally means 'peace' and 'security' and so a true Muslim is a person who is himself peaceful and who strives to establish peace and harmony in the world.

Preface

On Saturday 5 October 2019, the Worldwide Head of the Ahmadiyya Muslim Community, the Fifth Khalifah (Caliph), His Holiness, Hazrat Mirza Masroor Ahmad[aba] addressed an audience of dignitaries and guests on the second day of the 27th Annual Convention of the Ahmadiyya Muslim Community in France.

In this address His Holiness speaks about how the teachings of Islam safeguards the rights and freedoms of all people and how, by acting upon these teachings, lasting peace in society can be achieved. He further illustrates, contrary to the actions of so-called Muslim extremists, that the holy person of the Prophet of Islam[sas] was a champion in establishing and protecting universal rights. In great detail he draws a parallel between the verses of the Holy Qur'an and the practice of the Holy Prophet Muhammad[sas] in embedding such teachings into the fabric of a true Islamic society.

ISLAM - SAFEGUARDING RIGHTS AND FREEDOMS

All distinguished guests, *Assalamo Alaikum Wa Rahmatullah Wa Barakatohu*, peace and blessings of Allah be upon you all. First of all, I would like to thank all of our guests for having joined us at today's event, which is a purely religious function, organised by a Muslim community.

In recent years, the horrific and brutal atrocities of certain so-called Muslim groups have caused immeasurable levels of pain and anguish in different countries, including here in France. Such attacks can only be condemned in the strongest possible terms and our prayers and sympathies are always with the victims of such heinous crimes.

The true teachings of Islam have nothing to do with terrorism and extremism; rather, Islam is a religion of peace, love, tolerance and reconciliation. The word Islam literally means *peace* and *security* and so a true Muslim is a person who is himself peaceful and who strives to establish peace and harmony in the world. At a very basic level, Muslims are instructed to greet other people, be they Muslims or non-Muslims, with the words *Assalamo Alaikum* which mean *peace be upon you*.

This Islamic greeting is a gesture of goodwill, conveying peace and security to the recipient. Indeed, I have seen many non-Muslims, who have Muslim friends or acquaintances, who also choose to greet them in the Islamic way by offering peace of *salam*.

Anyway, it simply cannot be that our faith teaches us to receive every person with a message of peace and security, and at the same time, it requires us to usurp their rights, to oppose them or violently take up arms against them. It is impossible that Islam could have such contradictory teachings.

Therefore, let it be clear that all forms of extremism and violence are completely against Islam's teachings. To understand the true nature of Islam, it is important to reflect upon the time of the Founder of Islam, the Holy Prophet Muhammad (peace and blessings of Allah be upon him).

When he claimed to be a prophet of God, he and his followers were subjected to relentless and barbaric persecution. A few of the early Muslims were from relatively well-off and well-regarded families, but the vast majority were poorer members of society, including slaves. In order to intimidate and strike fear into them, the disbelievers of Makkah inflicted grievous and brutal cruelties upon them. However, the Prophet of Islam (peace and blessings of Allah be upon him) withstood the inhumane treatment and the unrelenting injustices with unparalleled levels of patience and fortitude and counselled his followers to do the same. For example, on one occasion, the Holy Prophet Muhammad (peace and blessings of Allah be upon him) observed a Muslim husband and wife and their young son being beaten and tortured by non-Muslims. Despite the merciless abuse and vicious torture, the Holy Prophet of Islam (peace and blessings of Allah be upon him) urged them to show restraint and to endure the horrific violence with patience. He neither instructed them to retaliate and nor did he invite his other followers to come and fight back against the non-Muslims; rather, he called on his followers to remain peaceful, even if it meant they lost their lives, and he reassured them that their reward lay in the hereafter in the loving arms of Allah the Almighty.[1]

Thereafter, the Prophet of Islam (peace and blessings of Allah be upon him) and his companions continued to endure the relentless oppression for many years, until finally they migrated to the city of Madinah so that they could practice their religion freely and live in peace.

However, it was not long before the disbelievers of Makkah pursued the Muslims to their new home and waged war against them. It was then that for the very first time, Allah the Almighty permitted the Muslims to fight back and this permission is mentioned in chapter 22, verses 40 to 41 of the Holy Quran.

In these verses, Allah the Almighty proclaimed that permission to fight was granted, because the Muslims were being attacked by people who sought not only the elimination of Islam, but who sought to destroy the institution of religion itself. The Quran says that if the Muslims were not permitted to fight back, then no church, synagogue, temple, mosque or the place of worship of any religion would remain safe. Hence, when the Holy Prophet of Islam (peace and blessings of Allah be upon him) and his followers were forced to partake in wars and battles, it was for the sake of defending the rights of all people. It was to ensure that Christians, Jews, Hindus, Muslims and the people of other faiths and beliefs had the right to worship as they pleased. If, as is often alleged, Islam permitted Muslims to spread its teachings violently, to conquer lands, and to try to eliminate other religions, then why would the Holy Quran explicitly state that it was the religious duty of Muslims to protect all religions and to safeguard the rights of their followers?

The reality is that the early Muslims gave their lives in order to establish and enshrine, once and for all, the principles of individual liberty, freedom of religion and freedom of belief. These freedoms are the cornerstones of the Islamic faith and have been preserved eternally in the Holy Quran, which has categorically declared in chapter 2, verse 257 that *"there should be no compulsion in religion"*. What a clear and unequivocal statement in defence of freedom of thought, freedom of religion and freedom of conscience. The Holy Quran teaches that religion is a personal matter for each individual and no one has the right to compel or coerce other people in this regard.

During the time of the Prophet of Islam (peace and blessings of Allah be upon him) and his four rightly guided Caliphs, the rights of non-Muslims were never usurped and nor were they pressured into accepting Islam or abandoning their traditions and beliefs. At every moment of his life, the Holy Prophet Muhammad (peace and blessings of Allah be upon him) sought peace and promoted inter-faith dialogue, mutual understanding and respect between the people of different communities. For example, after migrating to Madinah, he formed a treaty with the Jewish community and together they formed a system of government in which the Prophet of Islam (peace and blessings of Allah be upon him) was mutually chosen as the head of state.

According to the terms of the covenant, the Muslims and the Jews pledged to cooperate and to be faithful citizens of the state. The treaty guaranteed the right of every individual to practice their religion and customs without fear of persecution or sanction.

Never once did the Prophet of Islam (peace and blessings of Allah be upon him) deviate from the terms of the covenant. On the other hand, there were some instances when the non-Muslims violated the treaty and they were sanctioned according to the pre-existing terms. Islam has never permitted its followers to spread their faith through the use of force and nor does it permit Muslim governments or leaders to claim that only Muslims are permitted to live in their society.

As I have mentioned, under the terms of the Treaty of Madinah, all people were free to practice their traditions and beliefs. That society was bound together by one overriding principle, that irrespective of their religious beliefs, all members of society were duty-bound to be loyal citizens of the state and to refrain from all activities that could undermine the peace and security of society. Most certainly, during that era, Madinah was a model of pluralism, tolerance and a shining example of a thriving, multi-cultural society. Therefore, it would be entirely unjust to blame Islam for the misguided and malevolent conduct of the tiny minority of Muslims who defy its peaceful teachings.

Those individuals or groups who become radicalised and who seek to fulfil their own interests through extremism and terrorism have nothing to do with Islam. They may try to justify their hate-filled acts in Islam's name but all they do is defame and besmirch the noble and peaceful teachings of the Holy Quran and the Holy Prophet of Islam (peace and blessings of Allah be upon him).

From cover to cover, the Holy Quran is replete with enlightened guidance that instructs Muslims to avail every opportunity for attaining peace in the world.

For example, chapter 43, verses 89 to 90 describe the anguished and grief-stricken prayers of the Prophet of Islam (peace and blessings of Allah be upon him) in which he supplicated to Allah the Almighty that the message of truth and compassion that he presented to his people was being rejected. In reply, Allah the Almighty instructed him to turn aside and to continue to offer peace to others. The Arabic word *Amina* used, means to believe and to impart peace and so Allah the Almighty instructed the Holy Prophet Muhammad (peace and blessings of Allah be upon him) to convey the message of Islam and thereafter to leave the matter in the hands of God and to continue to bestow peace on those who rejected him.

Allah the Almighty reassured His Prophet (peace and blessings of Allah be upon him) that a time would come when those who rejected his teachings would recognise its truth.

The Holy Quran never once advocated violence or force against those who shunned its teachings; rather, it called on the Muslims to exhibit tolerance and patience. Therefore, if today, so-called Muslims or so-called Islamic governments manifest extremism or fanaticism, the blame lays squarely with them.

Their deceitful and abhorrent behaviour, through which the peace and harmony of the world is being shattered, can never be justified or excused in any way. Islam's teachings are categorical that violent conquest or forceful conversion are strictly prohibited. Indeed, any act or conduct that is detrimental to the peace and security of society is forbidden. At every juncture, the Prophet of Islam (peace and blessings of Allah be upon him) manifested compassion and benevolence.

He taught that a true Muslim is he from whose tongue and hand all others are safe.[2] He did not differentiate by saying that Muslims should be sympathetic and kind to Muslims alone, rather he made it clear that they must protect and care for all members of society, irrespective of their differences of belief.

Consequently, terrorists who commit suicide bombings, attack nightclubs, concert halls or stadiums or manically drive vehicles into members of the public are all guilty of violating the teachings of Islam in the most ghastly and barbaric fashion.

Apart from enshrining freedom of belief as a core human

right, the Holy Quran has also given many guiding principles for day-to-day life through which people can live together peacefully, irrespective of their different backgrounds or beliefs. For example, chapter 2, verse 189 of the Holy Quran lays down the principles for fair-trading and ensuring the integrity of all financial relationships or transactions.

In this verse, Allah the Almighty has instructed Muslims that they must never acquire wealth or property through means of deception; rather, Muslims are taught to be honest, trustworthy and to uphold the truth so that grievances and malice do not develop between different parties.

Islam teaches that unfair dealing and unjust trading weakens the unity within society and destroys its peace. Certainly, at a time when so much of the world's disorder and suffering, both at an individual and a collective level, is based upon selfishness and greed, the principles of equity and justice are crucial to maintaining peace within society. Furthermore, in chapter 83, verses 2-4, the Holy Quran states:

"Woe unto those who give short measure. Those who, when they take by measure from other people, take it full; but when they give by measure to others or weigh to them, they give them less."

These verses affirm that those who are exploitative in business transactions, who try to short-change others, whilst demanding more than their dues in return and who resort to deception and fraud, are cursed and will be disgraced.

The Holy Quran has also given detailed guidance regarding international relations and resolving internal conflicts or those that arise between nations. The Islamic focus is always on establishing sustainable peace and eliminating enmities and rivalries. For example, chapter 49, verse 10 of the Holy Quran states that if two parties or nations are in conflict then their neighbours, or neutral parties, should seek to bring about reconciliation through mediation and negotiations.

Those who intervene must remain impartial, rather than trying to settle the outcome in their own best interest. If peace cannot be established through dialogue, or if any party subsequently violates the terms of a negotiated settlement, then the other nations should unite against whosoever is perpetrating injustice and use force to stop them.

Once the aggressors adopt peace, they should not be humiliated and nor should unfair sanctions be levied upon them; rather, in the interests of fairness and long-term peace, they should be permitted to move forward as a free society and given whatever support is required to rebuild their nation. I believe that this outstanding Quranic principle is not just of value to Muslims, but is a universal principle for dispute resolution and if acted upon, can prove a means of stabilising the world and developing lasting peace.

Most regrettably, many Muslim countries fail to abide by this Quranic injunction and as a result, they continue to be embroiled in senseless conflicts and seem perpetually engaged in a cycle of violence and injustice.

As mentioned, this verse also makes it clear that once peace has been achieved, the victors should not seek to crush or humiliate the defeated party. The wisdom in this is clear to see. Peace will not last if a vanquished nation is demeaned in any way, rather frustrations and grievances are bound to emerge amongst its leaders and public.

Conversely, trust and mutual respect will develop if the defeated nation is treated with compassion and justice. However, today we repeatedly see that in the name of establishing peace, cruelties and injustices are perpetrated by dominant powers causing restlessness and animosity to develop. It means that any peace deal or truce hangs by the most delicate of threads and is constantly at risk of breaking down.

Such instability is of benefit to no one except terrorist and extremist groups, who prey on the frustrations of people and we have seen the consequences of this for many years.

In both the East and the West, the blue skies of peace and prosperity have given way to heavy clouds of war and injustice. Across much of the world, nations are being torn apart by dissension, revenge-seeking and a desire to degrade others. This state of unrest will continue to increase, until and unless international relations are based upon justice and integrity and fulfilling the rights of others. As I observe the world today, I can only pray that mankind does not continue to repeat the mistakes of the past.

Instead, let us learn from history, so we can build a better future for ourselves and for our coming generations.

If we look back to the period after the First World War, the League of Nations was formed, but it failed miserably in its task to maintain post-war peace. The reason for its failure was that justice and fairness did not prevail, rather alliances and blocs were allowed to form and certain nations were treated unreasonably and deprived of their dignity.

As a result, the most deadly war in the history of mankind, the Second World War, soon erupted. After six more devastating and chastening years of bloodshed, the war finally came to an end and the United Nations was established to maintain and preserve the peace and security of the world. Despite its lofty goals and stated ambitions, the United Nations has also failed in its mission. Today, once again, blocs are rapidly forming, society is becoming polarised and rifts between nations are deepening by the day. Many countries, Muslim and non-Muslim, do not seem to comprehend the true value of peace or to recognise the dangers that lie ahead.

Certainly, the consequences of warfare today are potentially far deadlier than anything we have ever seen before because several nations have developed nuclear weapons.

If any of those countries ever use the deadly weapons at their disposal they will not just be destroying the world as we know it, but will be ensuring that we leave behind the most horrific and devastating legacy for our children. If a nuclear war breaks out, generations of children will be born with mental and physical disabilities and so instead of contributing to their nations, they will live miserable existences and be a strain on society. Their homes will be filled with despair. Their towns will be filled with grief. And their nations will be consumed by misery. They will be justified in cursing us for engaging in such selfish and senseless warfare that shattered their dreams even before they were born.

Thus, no one should be under the illusion that this world crisis we are passing through is trivial or something that will heal itself without us changing our behaviour.

Furthermore, the instability of the world will continue to increase if the blame for the world's lack of peace and security continues to be laid at the door of Islam. Attacking a religion or its followers will only aggravate divisions.

It will embolden extremists on all sides to rise above the surface and to further their efforts of stoking the flames of hatred between the people of different communities and beliefs. As I have made it clear, if Muslim countries or terrorist groups perpetrate atrocities or cruelties in the name of Islam, it is because they have disregarded their religious teachings and seek only to fulfil their vested interests. Today's conflicts and wars have nothing to do with religion, rather they are all about attaining wealth, power and geo-political dominance. In light of this, I pray from the depths of my heart that may the people of the world join together for the common good and work with a spirit of unity and foster mutual trust and understanding.

Instead of blaming religion or pointing the finger at one another, let us focus all our energies on ensuring peace and leaving behind a safer world for those who follow us. Let it be that our future generations come to remember us with love and affection, rather than with hate and resentment. May every person and every nation come to fulfil the rights of one another and may justice and compassion prevail over all forms of injustice and conflict. With these words, I thank you all once again for joining us today. Thank you very much.

ISLAM & EUROPE - A CLASH OF CIVILISATIONS?

BERLIN, GERMANY
22 OCTOBER 2019

Speaking to an audience comprising more than 80 dignitaries and influential guests, including Members of the Bundestag (Parliament), diplomats, academics, faith leaders and representatives of the media, whilst standing just a few hundred metres from the Brandenburg Gate at the Adlon Kempinski Hotel, His Holiness directly addressed the common allegation that the presence of Islam and Muslims is a threat to Western civilisation and culture. Prior to the keynote address, several distinguished speakers took to the stage and spoke of their admiration of the Ahmadiyya Muslim Community and its efforts to propagate Islam's message of peace across the world, as well as its commitment to serving humanity.

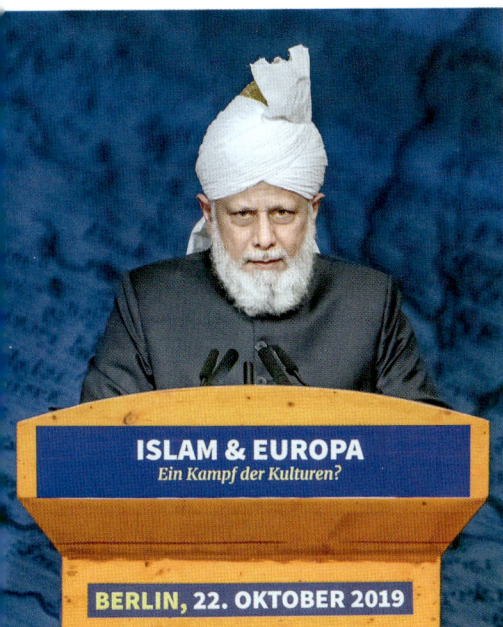

"

As a Muslim leader, I believe you should protect your heritage and culture by focusing your energies on arresting the decline in religion and bringing people back towards faith and belief, whether that be Christianity, Judaism or any other. It should not be that in the name of advancement, those values and moral standards that have been part of society for many centuries are suddenly abandoned.

Preface

On 22 October 2019, His Holiness - Hazrat Mirza Masroor Ahmad[aba] delivered a landmark and historic address in the heart of Berlin, entitled Islam and Europe: A Clash of Civilisations?

Prior to the keynote address, several distinguished speakers spoke of their admiration of the Ahmadiyya Muslim Community and its efforts to propagate Islam's message of peace across the world, as well as its commitment to serving humanity.

In this address, delivered three decades after a famous symbol of division, the Berlin Wall was knocked down, His Holiness urges today's leaders and governments to demolish the walls of hatred and conflict that have plagued modern society. Speaking to an audience comprising of more than 80 dignitaries and influential guests, including Members of the Bundestag (Parliament), diplomats, academics, faith leaders and representatives of the media, whilst standing just a few hundred metres from the Brandenburg Gate, His Holiness directly addresses the common misconception that the presence of Islam is a threat to Western civilisation and culture.

ISLAM & EUROPE - A CLASH OF CIVILISATIONS?

Bismillahir Rahmanir Raheem - In the Name of Allah, the Gracious, the ever Merciful.

All distinguished guests, *Assalamo Alaikum Wa Rahmatullahe Wa Barakatohu* - peace and blessings of Allah be upon you all.

First of all, I would like to take this opportunity to thank all of our guests who have accepted our invitation and joined us here this evening. In the world today, particularly in Western and developed nations, there is a great deal of heated debate about immigration and its effect on societies. Much of the debate centres around Muslims - because a view has developed that there is an unbridgeable divide between Muslims and other members of society.

Certain governments and members of the public fear a clash of civilisations and believe that Muslims are a threat to their society and cannot integrate into the Western world. Before responding to this contention, it is important to define what exactly is meant by *civilisation*? In this regard, I present the definition given by the Second Head of the Ahmadiyya Muslim Community, which I fully concur with.[1] According to the definition, civilisation is the material progress and development of a society. Factors that indicate the strength of a civilisation include its economic progress, the level of technological innovation, the advancement of the means of travel, communication and the intellectual progress of the society. For example, modern forms of communication and transportation are one marker of the level of civilisation, as are its financial system, its economy, its law and order, its trade and industry, the standards of its scientific and academic research and its overall educational standards. Furthermore, the efforts of a nation to foster peace and stability, whether by virtue of its law enforcement and military proficiency or by other means is also a measure of its civilisation.

Separate and distinct from civilisation is a nation's culture. Culture is a manifestation of the views of a people, their attitudes towards social issues and their practices and instead of being based on material progress, culture is rooted in morality and the religious values and traditions of a nation. Thus, civilisation is the material, technological and intellectual development of a society, whereas its culture is based on the religious, moral and philosophical make-up of that society.

The difference between civilisation and culture can be easily understood if we look back to the early period of Christianity. At that time, the Roman Empire was at the peak of its powers and, even now, it is considered as one of the greatest civilisations in the history of the world. Due to their material prosperity, urbanisation and the way its territories were governed, the Romans were considered to be tremendously civilised and educated.

However, their sophistication did not equate to higher standards of morality; rather, it was during the early period of Christianity that their people were infused with a progressive culture. Christianity gave people guiding principles based on religion and morality, whilst the Romans prescribed worldly laws and limits.

Hence, the progress and advancement of the Romans reflected their great civilisation, whereas Christianity gave the people a laudable culture. Over time, Christianity became the predominant religion of the Roman Empire and so the culture it established was adopted by a great civilisation. Allied together their supreme influence laid the foundations for the values and traditions that remain today in the West.

Whilst people in the West are moving away from religion, the basic moral values that underpin Western society remain those given by Christianity.

Regarding the debate about immigration, in recent decades, the demographics of several Western countries has altered. Immigrants have arrived from many countries, but it has been the influx of Muslims that has caused most concern and alarm. Many indigenous people fear that mass immigration from Muslim countries threatens their civilisation, culture and values, which have existed for many centuries.

As I have explained, we consider civilisation to be the material progress and advancement of society and rather than disapprove, oppose or deny the growth and development in the West, developing nations seek to emulate it. As a result, rather than Western civilisation being cast aside, we are seeing the opposite.

Due to the modern means of travel and communication, the world has become a global village. The advent of television, mass media and particularly the internet have meant that nothing now remains hidden in the world and so people who live in economically deprived countries can see how those in affluent nations live. They are being influenced by Western civilisation and desire to attain similar levels of material advancement and innovation.

Thus, the assertion that Western or European civilisation is threatened by the presence of Muslims does not hold water; rather, Western civilisation is influencing other parts of the world and this includes the Muslim world. On the other hand, a fear that the religious and moral culture of the West could be threatened if Islam spreads in Europe is a more legitimate concern and I shall now address this point.

Firstly, it is undeniable that people are rapidly moving away from religion and this trend is particularly acute in the West. In Western countries, whenever a census is conducted it shows that people are less and less inclined towards religion or belief in God. Given this, I believe that the rapid increase of atheism is a far greater threat to Western culture than Islam. Western values are centuries old and are based upon its religious traditions and especially on its Christian and Jewish heritage. However, these religious values and cultural norms are under attack from those who oppose all forms of religion and faith.

So, as a Muslim leader, I believe you should protect your heritage and culture by focusing your energies on arresting the decline in religion and bringing people back towards faith and belief, whether that be Christianity, Judaism or any other. It should not be that in the name of advancement, those values and moral standards that have been part of society for many centuries are suddenly abandoned.

I also believe that the decline in religion in the West is the main reason people fear Islam, because they know that, broadly speaking, Muslims remain attached to their faith. In light of this, I wish to make it clear that, despite what you hear or read in the media, there is no cause to fear Islam. Muslims believe the Holy Quran to be a final and perfect religious teaching and it is due to our love and obedience to the Holy Quran that we firmly believe that religion is a matter of the heart and personal to every individual.

In chapter 2, verse 257, the Holy Quran has categorically stated that there should be no compulsion in matters of religion. Therefore, there is no need for non-Muslims to fear that Muslims will try to forcefully spread their beliefs or impose their views on this part of the world. The hateful ideology of the tiny minority of so-called Muslims who have adopted extremism bears no correlation with the teachings of the Holy Quran. Indeed, I have said many times that governments and the relevant authorities should deal very firmly with extremists, be they Muslims or non-Muslims.

In terms of the Ahmadiyya Muslim Community, we believe that under no circumstances does Islam permit the use of force or any type of coercion in the spread of faith. Why then is there a need to fear Islam? Why do people think that their civilisation or culture is at risk from Muslims?

Now, after explaining the differences between civilisation and culture from an Islamic perspective, I would like to present some of the core teachings of Islam. Many myths and misconceptions about Islam and its Founder (peace and blessings of Allah be upon him) have spread and whilst it is not possible to cover all aspects of Islamic teachings in the short time available, I would like to mention some of the rights of mankind that Islam has established. A very significant verse of the Holy Quran, in terms of human rights, is chapter 4, verse 37 which states:

"And worship Allah and associate naught with Him, and show kindness to parents, and to kindred, and orphans, and the needy, and to the neighbour who is a kinsman and the neighbour who is a stranger, and the companion by your side, and the wayfarer and those whom your right hands possess…"

In this verse, where Allah the Almighty instructs Muslims to worship Him, He also instructs them to treat their parents with love and affection. How can this teaching, requiring Muslims to love and honour their parents clash with any religion or nation? How can such a teaching undermine Western society? The verse also requires Muslims to treat their relatives and loved ones with kindness and consideration. It requires them to support and comfort the most vulnerable and under-privileged members of society, such as orphans.

In this regard, we believe that one of the key ways to help the poor is through education. If younger members of society, who are from broken homes or who are stricken by poverty are educated, it will enable them to break free from the shackles of destitution. Opportunities will open up to them and so, free from frustration and resentment, such youths will grow to be productive members of society, rather than being lured towards a life of crime or gang culture. This is why, the Ahmadiyya Muslim Community lays great emphasis on education and within our limited resources, we have built schools in various African countries and fund scholarships for students who cannot afford higher education.

We also believe that rich countries should help the weaker nations of the world build solid foundations. If poorer countries can build up their economies and infrastructures, their people will have opportunities at home and have far less reason to migrate abroad. If their nations are stable and prosperous, it naturally follows that the region and the wider world will benefit.

In the aforementioned verse of the Holy Quran, special mention is made to fulfilling the rights of one's neighbours, whether they are Muslim or non-Muslims and it defines the scope of neighbours to be extremely wide.

The Prophet of Islam (peace and blessings of Allah be upon him) said that God Almighty had emphasised the rights of neighbours so strongly that he came to think neighbours would be included amongst a person's rightful heirs.[2]

Furthermore, in Islam, neighbours are not only those who live nearby but also those who live further afield, travel companions, work colleagues, subordinates and many other people besides. In effect, Allah the Almighty has made it a moral imperative for Muslims to fulfil the rights of all members of society.

The Founder of Islam (peace and blessings of Allah be upon him) also taught that a person who is not grateful to his fellow human beings, cannot be grateful to Allah the Almighty.[3] What a beautiful principle! Thus, it is necessary that alongside the worship of God, a Muslim must fulfil the rights of humanity.

Again, I would ask how can such a teaching be a threat to Western civilisation? These Islamic teachings are the means of cultivating peace and stability in society and can only help advance economic output and social development.

Hence, in my view, it is counter-productive for Western people to suggest that Islam or Muslims have no place in this part of the world.

If Muslims come here seeking to integrate, to fulfil the rights of neighbours and strive for the peace and betterment of society, then surely this is something to praise, rather than to condemn or castigate.

Moving on, some people argue or believe that Muslims are

instructed to perform Jihad and so they fear they will come to the West and wage a violent war seeking to enforce an Islamic civilisation and culture and shatter the peace of society. This is based on a clear misunderstanding of what Jihad is and why religious wars were fought in the early period of Islam. Islam is not a bloodthirsty or violent religion.

During the early period of Islam, the Muslims were forced to defend themselves after war was waged upon them and so a companion of the Holy Prophet Muhammad (peace and blessings of Allah be upon him) asked to join the Muslim army so he could take part in Jihad. The Prophet of Islam (peace and blessings of Allah be upon him) rejected his plea and said that, because his parents were in a fragile state, he should remain at home, care for them and consider that to be his Jihad.[4] If the objective of Jihad was conquest, bloodshed and warfare, the Prophet of Islam (peace and blessings of Allah be upon him) would surely have taken up his offer and sought to bolster the Muslim army.

I should clarify that, whilst it is true that Muslim armies fought in some religious wars during the early period of Islam, the purpose was never to overpower, oppress or compel people to accept Islam. Those wars were fought to protect the institution of religion and uphold principle of freedom of belief.

In chapter 22, verses 40-41, the Holy Quran very clearly states that if the aggressors were not stopped, all churches, synagogues, temples, mosques and other places of worship would be under grave threat, as the underlying intention of the disbelievers of

Makkah was to destroy all traces of religion from the face of the earth. This proves that Islam protects all religions.

Then, with regard to bringing up our children, chapter 6 verse 152 of the Holy Quran states that Muslims must not *"slay their children"*. This commandment instructs Muslims to nourish their children with love and affection, to morally guide them and to educate them so that they grow to become highly competent and moral individuals who are assets to their community and nation.

Similarly, Islam has taught Muslims to defend the rights of vulnerable members of society. For example, in chapter 4, verse 7 of the Quran, Muslims are obliged to protect orphan children from exploitation and to guard their inheritance with integrity, until they reach an age where they can manage it themselves.

Furthermore, another very common allegation in the Western world is that Muslims do not respect women or their rights. First of all, it should be noted that Islam was the first religion to give women the right to inherit, the right to divorce and various other rights. In addition, Islam emphasises the vast importance of educating girls and giving them opportunities for personal growth and development. Not a single girl or woman should ever be deprived of education or discriminated against in any respect.

In an era, when the rights of women and girls were routinely disregarded, and they were regarded as inferior to boys, the Prophet of Islam (peace and blessings of Allah be upon him) brought a revolution in the cause of women's rights. He instructed Muslims to love, cherish and respect their daughters and to never consider them lesser to their sons.

Moreover, in a famous saying, the Holy Prophet of Islam (peace and blessings of Allah be upon him) said that *"paradise lies under the feet of one's mother"*.[5] These words illustrate the momentous role women play in society and their unique and distinguished status in society.

Primarily, it is the role of mothers to nurture their children through their formative years and so they play the leading role in ensuring that the coming generations grow into morally upstanding citizens who contribute to their society.

Mothers are the people who have the power and influence to turn their nations into a heaven on earth and who can unlock the doors to an eternal Paradise for their children.

Furthermore, in chapter 4, verse 20, the Holy Quran has stated that Muslim men must treat their wives lovingly and respectfully. In Western countries, not a day goes by without reports of the police or the courts being forced to intervene and deal with horrifying cases of domestic abuse. Various studies and reports, such as the 2018 report by the Office for National Statistics in the UK, prove that such crimes are not linked to any religion and another recent report has shown that the same is true here in Germany. Thus, it is entirely unjust to brand Islam as a misogynistic religion.

As I have outlined, Islam is a religion that bestows honour and dignity upon women and any man who treats a woman cruelly is guilty of grievously violating Islam's teachings.

Islam also requires its followers to respect the religious sentiments and beliefs of other people. The Covenant of Madinah was a true illustration of this teaching where the Torah was recognised and respected as the law-bearing book of the Jews.

Islam has even established the rights of a person's enemies and opponents, whereby chapter 2, verse 191 of the Holy Quran states that no injustice or transgression should be done against one's enemy, even during a state of war. Regrettably, in today's world, which proudly boasts of being more civilised and advanced than any previous era, individuals and countries disregard the rights of their opponents as a matter of routine and perpetrate huge cruelties and waste no opportunity for revenge.

In chapter 5, verse 9 of the Holy Quran, Allah the Almighty has proclaimed that the enmity of a nation or people should never incite a person to sacrifice the principles of justice and equity; rather, Islam teaches that in all circumstances, no matter how challenging, you must remain firmly attached to the principles of justice and integrity and never be motivated by a desire for vengeance.

As a result of this magnificent teaching, we see the unparalleled example of grace, compassion and mercy exhibited by the Holy Prophet Muhammad (peace and blessings of Allah be upon him) at the time of the Victory of Makkah.

History proves that Muslims were killed, plundered and tortured in Makkah and ultimately, they were driven out of their homes and had to migrate.

Yet when he returned victoriously to Makkah and the entire city was under his command, his first pronouncement was that no revenge would be taken from those who had brutally persecuted the Muslims.

At that moment of triumph, the Holy Prophet Muhammad (peace and blessings of Allah be upon him) exhibited supreme humility and forbearance.

He declared that, in accordance with Islam's teachings, all those who had tormented the Muslims were to be instantly forgiven and that nobody would be treated unjustly, regardless of whether they accepted Islam or not.

Another moral revolution in favour of the weakest members of society brought by Islam regarded slavery, which prior to Islam, was rampant and considered a normal part of society. Upon the command of Allah the Almighty, the Prophet of Islam (peace and blessings of Allah be upon him) sought to bring an end to this practice.

Thus, chapter 24, verse 34 the Holy Qur'an states that if a slave seeks freedom, he should be released and if certain fiscal dues are levied, they must be reasonable and payable in small, easily manageable installments or be waived altogether.

As I said, during that era, slavery was part and parcel of society and so by calling for their emancipation, the Prophet of Islam (peace and blessings of Allah be upon him) brought about a sea-change in attitudes.

In today's world, physical slavery no longer exists, but it has been replaced by economic bondage and servitude, wherein the relationship between the most powerful nations on earth and weaker countries has become akin to the relationship of a master and a slave. For example, loans disguised as aid-packages are given by rich countries to weaker nations who have no option but to accept whatever strings are attached.

Invariably, the crippling levels of interest mean that the short-term loans lead to long-term misery and liability. The end result is that the defaulting country has no choice but to bend to the will of the dominant nation. Such slavery is utterly immoral.

From the outset, Islam also established the rights of non-Muslims and counselled Muslims to show restraint for the sake of the peace and unity of society. For example, in chapter 6, verse 109, the Holy Quran declares that Muslims should not even speak against the idols of non-religious people, because it could provoke them to speak against Allah the Almighty.

Thus, to ensure tensions are not inflamed and to protect society from a vicious cycle of hatred and hostility, Muslims have been instructed to show patience at all times.

In the short time available, I have mentioned only a few points that illustrate the rights of humanity that have been established by Islam. I hope what I have said will have reassured you that Islam is not a threat to Western civilisation or its culture. If there are any Muslims who usurp the rights of non-Muslims, it is only because they reject Islam's teachings or are wholly ignorant of them. They dishonour Islam and serve only to defame its pure name.

In conclusion, it is clear we are living in a world that is on tenterhooks and I fear the precarious situation we are facing could escalate at any time. People must realise that words can have far-reaching consequences and so rather than speaking of a clash of civilisations, or needlessly ratcheting up tensions between different communities, people should refrain from attacking the religious teachings of one another.

Instead of seeking to place restrictions upon the expressions of faith, we should recognise that we are all part of one human race more connected than ever before. We should embrace our diversity and focus on establishing unity so that long-term peace can develop in the world.

However, currently we are seeing the opposite. Muslim and non-Muslim countries alike are putting their own interests ahead of the interests of the wider world and are crossing all limits of fairness and morality in pursuit of their goals. Reminiscent of the dark days of the past, opposing blocs and alliances are forming and it seems as though the world is hell-bent on inviting its destruction.

Today, there are a host of countries who have acquired nuclear bombs or other destructive weapons that have the potential to destroy civilisation as we know it. Who is to say that these weapons will never be used or will not end up in the wrong hands? All it takes is one miscalculation or misstep for hostilities to trigger the unthinkable. The consequences of such a war are incomprehensible but it is safe to say that the world will never be the same again.

If nuclear weapons are ever used, it will not just be us who bear the consequences; rather, our children and future generations will have to suffer for our sins. Generations of children will be born with intellectual and physical disabilities and have their hopes and dreams shattered through no fault of their own.

Is that the parting legacy we wish to bequeath to those who follow us? Surely not! Thus, instead of fanning flames of hatred, whether based on religious or ethnic differences or for political objectives, we must recognise the warning signs and change our ways before it is too late. Let us all, irrespective of our differences, join together and work with a spirit of mutual respect, tolerance and affection for the peace of the world and to promote freedom of belief.

May Allah grant wisdom and intelligence to those who are causing conflict in the name of religion and may peace and justice prevail – *Ameen*. With these words, I would like to thank you once again for joining us this evening.

Thank you very much.

References

The Need for outward and Inner Peace

1   *The Holy Qur'an* 2:139
2   *Sunan Ibn Majah*, Kitab-ul-Adab, Book 33, Hadith 37
3   *Sahih Bukhari*, Kitab-ul-Imaan, Book 2, Hadith 6
4   *The Holy Qur'an* 26:4
5   *Sunan Abi Dawood*, Kitab-ul-Jihad, Book 15, Hadith 138.
6   *World Faith*, Ruth Cranston. Harper & Brothers, 1949, p. 155
7   *The Holy Qur'an* 1:2

A Beacon of Light Spreading Compassion to All

1   *The Holy Qur'an* 2:257
2   *The Holy Qur'an* 9:107-110
3   *Al-Adab Al-Mufradat*, Kitab-ul-Jaar, Book 6, Hadith 9
4   *Sunan Ibn Majah*, Kitab-ul-Adab, Book 33, Hadith 18

Islam - Safeguarding Rights & Freedoms

1   Muhammad ibn Ishaq. *Sirat Rasul Allah*. Translated by Guillaume, *The Life of Muhammad*. Oxford University Press, 1955. p.145
2   *Sahih Muslim*, Kitab-ul-Iman, Book 1, Hadith 69

Islam & Europe: A Clash of Civilisations?

1 *Introduction to the Study of the Holy Qur'an*, Hazrat Mirza Bashir-ud-din Mahmood Ahmad, Islam International Publications Ltd, 2016, p. 14-15
2 *Sunan Ibn Majah*, Kitab-ul-Adab, Book 33, Hadith 18
3 *Sunan Abi Dawood*, Kitab-ul-Adab, Book 43, Hadith 39
4 *Sahih Bukhari*, Kitab-ul-Adab, Book 78, Hadith 3
5 *Sunan An-Nasa'i*, Kitab-ul-Jihad, Book 25, Hadith 20

Index